Object Talks for Any Day

by
Verna L.
Kokmeyer

STANDARD
PUBLISHING
Cincinnati, Ohio

To Steve, Christy, Kathy
Laurie, J.J.,
Andrea and Dan

Unless otherwise noted, all Scripture quotations in this book are from the *International Children's Bible, New Century Version,* copyright © 1986, 1988 by Word Publishing, Dallas, Texas 75039. Used by permission.

Verses marked TLB are taken from *The Living Bible,* copyright © 1971 by Tyndale House Publishers, Wheaton, Illinois. Used by permission.

02 01 00 99 98 97 96 95   5 4 3 2 1

ISBN 0-7847-0304-3

EARS AND MOUTH

THEME: Talking with God

OBJECT: A telephone

TEXT: Love the Lord your God. Obey him. Stay close
to him. *Deuteronomy 30:20*

APPLICATION:
Today I brought along a telephone. The receiver has a
part on each end of it. *(Point them out.)* Why does it need
two parts? *(One to talk into, and the other to hear out of.)*
To talk with someone on the telephone, we need to be able
to hear *and* speak, so the receiver has a place for an ear,
and a place for a mouth.

Have you ever tried to talk to someone on the phone
who does all the talking? You don't even need the mouth
part of your phone, because the person just goes on and
on. Do you like it when that happens? *(No.)* To get really
close to someone, both of you need to be able to share,
each having a time to talk and a time to listen.

If we don't like it when someone does all the talking, why
do we sometimes treat God that way? When we pray, we
unload all the problems we have on Him. Then we run off,
ignoring the ways He talks to us.

Do you know how God talks to us? *(Discuss.)* He tells us
in His Word how to live, and He sometimes talks by having
other Christians speak to us. Then, too, He often speaks
quietly to our hearts, and we know what He wants us to do.
To hear His voice, we have to listen.

Remember, just as the telephone has a place to talk and
a place to listen, so we should have times when we talk to
God, and other times when we listen.

PRAYER: May we spend time talking to You, O God, but
may we also take time to listen. Amen.

EQUAL SENSE

THEME: God sees the heart.

OBJECTS: Ten pennies, two nickels, one dime

TEXT: "God does not see the same way people see. People look at the outside of a person, but the Lord looks at the heart."   *1 Samuel 16:7*

APPLICATION:

Look at the money I brought along today: pennies, nickels and a dime. *(Show coins.)* On this pile we are going to put ten pennies. Over here we'll stack two nickels, and next to that is room for the dime. These piles look very different from each other. The penny pile is tall, and we can easily knock it down. The nickels are the biggest. The dime is short and small, and it's all by itself.

Which stack is worth more? *(Get response.)* It's true! Even though the piles don't look alike, they all have the same value. You could buy the same thing with any stack.

Like these coins, we all look very different from each other. Some of us are taller, some are shorter. Some of us are bigger than others. There are those who are easily hurt, like the stack of pennies that is easily knocked down. Some may prefer to be alone like the dime.

When God looks at us, He checks out what we are like inside. It doesn't matter how we are shaped, or what our personalities are like. What matters to the Lord is our love for Him and how we show that love. We may get caught up in how others look on the outside. How they are shaped and whether their shoes are Reebok or Nike can seem very important. We may even tease those who have different shapes, or wear clothes we would not wear. If we love Jesus, we must look inside others just as He does. Remember that like the coins, we all have equal value.

PRAYER: Lord, thank You that though we are different we are all special to You. Amen.

A SIGN TO CONSIDER

THEME: Consider God's wonders.

OBJECT: A stop sign, or a reproduction of one

TEXT: "Stop and notice God's miracles. Do you know how God controls the clouds and makes his lightning flash? God All-Powerful is too high for us to reach. He has great strength. He is always right and never punishes unfairly."

Job 37:14, 15, 23

APPLICATION:

The sign I brought along today is not my favorite. *(Show.)* What do we have to do when we see this sign? *(Stop.)* I don't always want to stop. Sometimes I'm late. Often I'm hungry and want to get home fast. If I slam on the brake, everything falls off the seat. Suppose I decide not to stop when I see this sign, and just go faster instead? *(Discuss: accident, getting stopped by police, costly.)*

We don't read about this kind of sign in the Bible, but the Bible does remind us to stop. We may be in a hurry to get somewhere. If everyone is hurrying and you stop fast, the person following may bump into you. Maybe it's more fun to spend time with friends, or watch a favorite TV show. Stopping is not a favorite thing to do.

Why do we need to stop anyway? *(Discuss.)* Just as it is dangerous not to stop when we are in a car, it is dangerous not to stop and take time to see what our Lord has made. What do you see when you stop and look? *(Discuss.)* Thinking about the beautiful things around us reminds us what God has made, and how great He is. It helps us know Him better, and love Him more.

When your car comes to a stop sign, stop and look both ways for cars. Other times, stop and look all ways. Spend time with God, who has made everything you see.

PRAYER: Stop us, Lord. When we see all the beautiful things You've made, we get to know You better. Amen.

OUT OF MY MOUTH

THEME: Watch what you say—you can't take it back.

OBJECTS: A tube of toothpaste, plate

TEXT: I hope my words and thoughts please you. Lord, you are my Rock, the one who saves me.   *Psalm 19:14*

APPLICATION:

There are a lot of ways to get toothpaste out of a tube. Some people neatly roll it from one end, forcing the toothpaste out the other end. Others squeeze the center. I want a volunteer to squeeze all the paste out of this tube. I don't care how it's done. We'll keep it from going all over by holding it over this plate. *(Choose a volunteer, and hold the plate while the tube is emptied.)*

Great job! That was part one. Now for part two. I need another volunteer. Are you ready? *(Get response from the volunteer.)* OK. Very carefully, I want you to put all the toothpaste back in the tube. *(Without pausing.)* I'll keep holding the plate for you. Let's see—I can maybe hold it on this side to make it easier. Can you reach that? Now, just carefully put it back in. *(Pause.)* Let me raise the plate. That should make it easier. Will that help? What? *(Have volunteer respond that it's impossible.)*

The toothpaste came out easier than we can put it back. Our words can be like that. They come out of our mouths quickly and without a lot of thought. Have you ever said something to someone and then wished you hadn't said it? Can you put the words back into your mouth after you said them? Just as it is impossible to put toothpaste back in the tube, it is impossible to take words back after they are said.

Thoughtless words can make someone cry. If spoken in anger, they make others feel bad and make us look bad. Once the words are out of our mouths, it's too late. That's why it is important to be careful what we say. Even our thoughts must be good, because words often show what we are thinking.

I've caught the toothpaste on the plate, so we didn't make a mess. Words can't be caught that way, and what we say can make a big mess.

Pray that our words and thoughts are those that are pleasing to God.

PRAYER: Lord, help us to think pure thoughts and speak words that You would like. Amen.

TWINS

THEME: Sorting out the truth

OBJECTS: Two similar plants, one real, one silk

TEXT: Lord, tell me your ways. Show me how to live. Guide me in your truth. Teach me, my God, my Savior.
Psalm 25:4, 5

APPLICATION:

I have two plants with me today. They look a lot alike. If I were to go on vacation, I'd have to leave careful instructions for my friends because my silk plant *(point out each)* might get watered right along with my real one.

It's not always easy to tell real things from fakes. In fact, sometimes the fake looks the best. This fake plant never gets brown, or drops leaves when it's dry.

Often we must decide what is truth and what is not. Life is full of fake things. We can easily be tricked by what people say, or how they look. A smooth-talking person may say things that we like to hear while someone who loves us will say the things we need to hear, even if they are hard to hear.

Just as my note would have helped friends to tell the real

plant from the fake, God helps us make decisions through His Word. God's Word tells us how people who love Jesus should act. If we know what the Bible says, we will be able to sort out right from wrong. Don't be fooled by fake things and liars—know what the Bible says and choose to believe the truth.

PRAYER: It is not always easy to tell truth from fake. Teach us Your truth. Amen.

RETURN TO SENDER

THEME: The Lord's faithfulness

OBJECT: Yo-yo

TEXT: When a man's steps follow the Lord, God is pleased with his ways. If he stumbles, he will not fall, because the Lord holds his hand.   *Psalm 37:23, 24*

APPLICATION:
Yo-yos are great toys. Put the string on a finger, and let the yo-yo move down and up. *(Demonstrate.)* I'm not good at this. If I were better, I could show you how the yo-yo could be made to do all sorts of things before returning to my hand. Most of the time my yo-yo just goes down and returns to my hand where it belongs.

All of us want to be kept in Jesus' hand. God promises to remain close to those who believe in Him. When we sin and do things that do not please God, it may seem like God is farther away, just like the yo-yo when it moves away from my hand *(demonstrate)*. If we tell God we are sorry, He is faithful to forgive our sins. God never gives up on us the way I sometimes give up on my yo-yo. God is good at taking care of us. He keeps close those who trust in Him.

PRAYER: Thank You for forgiving us when we do things that are bad, and for keeping us in Your hand. Amen.

TEAM SPIRIT

THEME: The Lord is our God.

OBJECTS: Various baseball caps, a cap with the name "Jesus" on it (can be paper pinned on)

TEXT: He is our God. And we are the people he takes care of and the sheep that he tends.   *Psalm 95:7*

APPLICATION:
A lot of people wear baseball caps. I brought along some of my favorites. *(Show caps.)* When I wear one I show that I like a certain sports team. If I went to a sports event, I would certainly wear a hat that told which side I was rooting for. I might have to change hats to go to a different game the next week. *(Change hats.)*

My favorite hat is this yellow and blue hat. *(Substitute your favorite team colors and put the hat on.)* See how it says, ("Let's Go Blue") on it? I am a (University of Michigan) fan, and probably would not change to another hat very quickly. My hat shows what team I support. I'd even wear it if I were the only (Michigan) fan around.

When my team does something special, I make sure everyone knows it. I feel a part of the team along with others who support the (University of Michigan) team.

Often the (Michigan) team wins, but sometimes it loses. That happens to most teams and it can be disappointing. People usually try to blame a loss on someone like the coach, or something like the weather.

I'd like to tell you about another team whose Leader never disappoints me. *(Put on "Jesus" hat.)* I don't usually wear a hat like this, but today I wanted you to think about what it means to have Jesus as our God, and to be one of His people.

As Christians we have others who are part of our team. Knowing someone is a Christian makes that person a friend, even more than the bond between me and someone else who wears a (Michigan) hat. Even if other Christians are not around, I should not be ashamed to let others know that I am on God's team.

When Jesus does something special in my life I should be excited about sharing the news with others. More people will want to be Christians when they see the care our Leader gives.

Keep on wearing baseball caps. When you put one on remember the other team you are a part of. Remember you belong to Jesus.

PRAYER: Lord, as part of Your team, may we be excited Christians. Amen.

OVERFLOWING PRAISE

THEME: Our lives should be overflowing with praises to God.

OBJECTS: Two cans of soda, floor covering if necessary (A good outdoor campfire lesson)

TEXT: Let me speak your praise.   *Psalm 119:171*

APPLICATION:

I like drinking pop (soda) from the can—especially on a very hot day. *(Open a can, and set it on a table.)* Have you ever opened a can for a drink? *(Pause.)* How do you get the pop out of the can? Yes, the pop comes out if you tip the can and take a drink. Unless you do that, the pop just stays in the can. What would happen to the pop if we just left it open on the table for a day or two? It wouldn't take long before all the fizz would be gone. The good news is that your eyes wouldn't water when you took a drink. The bad news is that it would taste re-al-ly blah.

But tell me *(confidentially),* have you ever given the can some good shakes, and then opened it? What happens? Yes! Let's try it. *(Shake.)* Get out of the way! *(Pause.)* Wait—we better not. I'm sorry, I get carried away. I love to be a part of exciting things. *(Pause.)* Maybe if I wait someone else will open it.

What? You want me to open it, even though I've shaken it? You're sure? You wouldn't rather go back to your seats? OK, get ready! Get out of the way, or it will spray on you too. *(Open can.)* Was that exciting or what? Wasn't it great just to be around all the excitement?

Did you know that God wants us to be that excited about Him? He doesn't want us to sit around not being used. He wants us to be "shook up" about Him. Our hearts should be bubbling over with joy. Too often we wait around for someone else to get excited.

Do you think if I tried—maybe put my thumb over the hole—I could have kept the pop in the can? No way! It should be just as impossible to keep our praise for Jesus inside us.

That kind of excitement spills all over everyone. You didn't want to leave until you saw what the pop in the can would do. If you're excited about Jesus, your friends won't want to leave before learning what Jesus will do in their lives.

Get excited about Jesus. Let your praise overflow!

PRAYER: O God, may we be so excited about You that our praise overflows. Amen.

NOWHERE FAST

THEME: We need God's power.

OBJECT: Stationary exercise bike

TEXT: If the Lord doesn't build the house, the builders are working for nothing.   *Psalm 127:1*

APPLICATION:
This kind of bike is very popular and I thought it would be fun to bring one here. Let's put it here in the center front. You can watch me ride right down the aisle (across the room) and out the back door. OK, time to get moving. *(Get on.)* Yep, pedaling isn't difficult at all. Not much is happening though. Shall I pedal faster? Whew! It's a good thing I ate a good breakfast. This isn't as easy as it looks.

I'm not moving at all. Wait a minute. . . wait a minute. I'll just get it started a little. *(Get off and drag bike six inches ahead. Then return to pedaling.)* Hmm. The speedometer says I'm going fifty miles an hour, but I'm no closer to the back door. No matter how hard I work, it doesn't make a difference.

This is how it can be with my life. I work very hard on some projects but don't seem to get anywhere. Why? The Bible tells me that unless the Lord works with me, all my work is as useless as the pedaling of this bike. The bike isn't made to move ahead by itself. Neither am I.

Just as I can pedal hard and go nowhere on my bike, I can work hard in life and get nowhere. Without the Lord's blessing nothing will happen. I can work harder and faster, but it won't make a difference. The Lord makes everything happen. Pray for His power in everything you do.

PRAYER: Thank You for Your power within us so we can serve You in wonderful ways. Amen.

MADE FOR HIS HAND

THEME: We are made to praise God.

OBJECT: M&M's candy

TEXT: I praise you because you made me in an amazing and wonderful way.   *Psalm 139:14*

APPLICATION:

You all know about my favorite candy. They are milk chocolate, covered with a thin candy shell. Do you need another hint? They're made to melt in your mouth, not in your hand. What kind of candy do I like? *(Show M&M's.)*

It's true that M&M's are made to melt in my mouth. Still, on a very hot day, after carrying the candy around for a while, I get colored spots in my hand. Has that happened to you? For the most part though, it isn't until I get M&M's in my mouth that the thin candy shell melts, and the chocolate oozes out. Yum! M&M's are worthless in the hand, but taste great when you throw them in your mouth.

M&M's are made to melt in your mouth. Do you know

what we are made to do? *(Discuss.)* We are made to praise God. Sometimes we don't praise Him as we are made to do. Like M&M's melting in the wrong place, we might get tired or hot—maybe even angry—and forget to praise Him. Instead of spots in the hand, our mistakes make stains that only Jesus can remove.

We are really useful only when we are doing what we were made to do. Let's all do what we were made for. Let's praise God.

PRAYER: You have made us to praise You. May we give You that praise. Amen.

HANG ON

THEME: Helping each other

OBJECT: A rope long enough for pupils to hold on to and walk single file

TEXT: Two people are better than one. . . . If one person falls, the other can help him up.   *Ecclesiastes 4:9, 10*

APPLICATION:

Today we're going for a walk. I'll lead, and the rest of you follow, holding on to the rope. *(Take a walk, if possible with corners and steps. You may wish to have some traveling music. With a wireless microphone you can make comments about how well they are walking together. End up where you started, and continue the message.)*

I noticed some things about our walk. When we turned corners, no one went the wrong way. Going the same direction was easy, because everyone held on to the rope. If you had trouble keeping up, friends carried you along. Did anyone trip? If you did, you didn't fall, because others were holding up the rope.

As Christians we need to be joined together—not by a rope, but by our love for Jesus. When we go in a wrong direction, doing things that are not good, our Christian friends help keep us on track. When we get tired, those next to us keep us going. We are less likely to trip, or make mistakes, because other Christians can remind us to stay close to Jesus.

It is important to have friends who love Jesus like we do. We can help each other live for Him. Life is easier when we walk with friends who know the love of Jesus.

PRAYER: Lord, we love You. Thanks for friends who help us live for You. Amen.

NAMED AND NUMBERED

THEME: God cares for us.

OBJECT: License plate

TEXT: "I will not forget you. See, I have written your name
on my hand."   *Isaiah 49:15, 16*

APPLICATION:

Every car has a license plate. Not only does it show the
name of the state the car comes from, but it also includes a
few numbers or letters that no other car has. Why do cars
need a license? *(Discuss.)* Yes, the license plate tells us
where the car belongs, and who owns it. If the car is lost or
stolen, the license number will help the police find the car
again, so they can put it safely back in the owner's garage.

People don't wear license plates. I'm glad, aren't you? I'd
hate to walk around with a number on my back. Yet, God
made each of us different from everyone else. Should we be
worried? Do you think He'll forget us, or get us mixed up?
(Discuss.)

We don't need license plates taped to our backs because
God knows each of us by name. The Bible says your name
is written in the palm of God's hand. How does that make
you feel? *(Special, loved, safe, etc.)*

We don't have to worry about getting lost, or being
taken away from God. He is right beside us. When He is in
our heart, He knows who we are, and that we belong to
Him. We are safe in His love.

PRAYER: It is very good to know we are special, and that
our names written in the palm of Your hand. Thank You
for Your love. Amen.

ERROR MAIL

THEME: Replacing the bad in our lives with good

OBJECT: Mailbox with a flag

TEXT: "I will take out the stubborn heart like stone from your bodies. And I will give you an obedient heart of flesh. I will put my Spirit inside you. And I will help you live by my rules."   *Ezekiel 36:26, 27*

APPLICATION:

Have you mailed any letters lately? I usually take my mail down to my own mailbox. I put in all the letters I'm ready to be rid of. Most of the time the envelopes contain payment for what I've done in the past. How do I let the mailman know that he needs to clean out the old outgoing mail before giving me new incoming mail? *(Discuss and demonstrate putting the flag up.)* When I'm ready to have old mail taken out so new can be put in, I put up the flag.

Just as the mailman cleans out the mailbox, our lives need to have the old sin taken away before there is room for Jesus. He pays the price for the sin in our lives, but doesn't take it away until we signal by asking for God's forgiveness. Then, like the bill payments taken out of my box, He takes away the sinful heart, and leaves a new heart full of love.

God's Spirit inside us helps us to obey God, and do what He wants us to do.

PRAYER: Lord, make this prayer our signal to You. Take away our sinful hearts, and give each of us a heart full of love. Amen.

TICKTOCK

THEME: Seek the Lord.

OBJECT: Clock with hands set at ten o'clock

TEXT: Plant the good seeds of righteousness and you will reap a crop of my love; plow the hard ground of your hearts, for now is the time to seek the Lord, that he may come and shower salvation upon you. *Hosea 10:12, TLB*

APPLICATION:

Today I've brought along a clock. Let's play a game. I'm going to set the hands, and you tell me what time is set on the clock.

What time is it when the big hand is on twelve, and the little hand is on ten? *(Ten o'clock.)* How about when the big hand is on six, and the little hand is on four? *(Four-thirty.)* You are really doing well, but I want you to think very carefully before you answer the next one. If you listened to our Scripture verse, you will know the answer.

Let's set the clock to the time it is right now. *(Do.)* The question is, what time is it? The Bible tells us, but it doesn't say that the time is *(current time)*. Do you remember what time it is according to today's verse? The Bible tells us that "now is the time to seek the Lord." Whether it is ten o'clock, or four o'clock, or even *(current time),* is not as important as whether or not you are seeking the Lord.

What does it mean to "seek the Lord"? Does the Lord ever get lost? *(No, people get lost.)* What are some things we can do to seek the Lord? *(Read our Bibles, listen to our parents and teachers, pray, sing praises, try to do everything to make God happy.)* Even if you can't tell time, you can know that "now is the time to seek the Lord."

PRAYER: Dear Jesus, I love You. I want to grow closer to You and know You better. Help me to remember that now is always the time to seek You. Amen.

FLAVORED WITH YOU

THEME: Make the world a better place.

OBJECTS: Two drinking glasses, two cups of sand or fine cat box filler, milk, chocolate milk mix and spoons

TEXT: "You are the salt of the earth. But if the salt loses its salty taste, it cannot be made salty again. It is good for nothing. It must be thrown out for people to walk on."

Matthew 5:13

APPLICATION:

Milk is OK, but I like it even better after I turn it into chocolate milk. I'll just add a little sand, and it will soon be the right color. *(Demonstrate mixing sand.)* Actually, I didn't want to go outside to get the sand, so I'm stirring in a little cat box filler. Who would like to try my chocolate milk? *(Pause.)* Why not?

To make something better, we have to add good stuff. I can get rid of this other stuff. *(Set aside sand, etc.)* Now let's try adding real chocolate. *(Demonstrate, adding chocolate to milk and drinking it.)* That's really good.

Chocolate can be mixed in milk to make it better. People who love Jesus are made to be mixed in the world to make it a better place. Only real Christians can change the world for better. If we are not like Jesus, we might as well be dumped out like the bad stuff I first put in my milk.

We need to add good flavor to our world. When our friends are mean, Jesus helps us to be kind to them and love them out of their meanness. When someone is left out, Jesus wants us to be a friend. Even if we're very young, we can help others, and speak out when we see others being picked on. Chocolate changes milk. You can change the world by mixing in the flavor of Jesus.

PRAYER: Dear God, help us to flavor the world, making it a better place to be. Amen.

KNOW YOUR FRUIT

THEME: Marks of a Christian

OBJECTS: A bunch of real grapes, a similar-looking bunch of fake grapes

TEXT: "You will know these people because of the things they do. Good things don't come from bad people, just as grapes don't come from thornbushes . . . . You will know these false prophets by what they produce."

Matthew 7:16, 20

APPLICATION:

I brought along two bunches of grapes. They look alike, don't they? Yet they are very different from each other. Can you tell me how they are different?

Yes, this is fruit we can eat. It is juicy, delicious, and it gives us strength. The other bunch is make-believe. It may look good, but it is not useful for much of anything but a decoration. Yet we call both of these bunches "grapes."

A lot of people call themselves Christians. The Bible says you can tell Christians from people who are not Christians by their actions. Just as we can tell a good vine by the delicious grapes growing on it, we can know someone is a Christian by the good things he or she does. It is not for us to decide who is a Christian and who is not. God knows that. The important thing for us is to make sure *our* actions tell others that Jesus Christ lives in our hearts.

Can you tell me how a Christian acts? *(Discuss—kind, helpful, praises God, joyful, has peace, wants to share, etc.)* If we really love and follow Jesus, our actions will be like His. Think about it. Do you act like a Christian? It is important that we are not just saying or thinking we are Christians. If we love Jesus, everything we do should show we are like Him.

PRAYER: May we not just say we are Christians, but may we show we are like Jesus by our actions. Amen.

CLOSE UP

THEME: How to see God

OBJECT: Binoculars

TEXT: "I tell you the truth. Anything you did for any of my people here, you also did for me."   *Matthew 25:40*

APPLICATION:
(Start this lesson by spending some time just looking around with binoculars.) No, I don't see Him there. Hmm. He doesn't seem to be there either. That's strange. I thought these binoculars made everything easier to see. I thought I'd see Jesus here. Do you think if I keep looking I'll see Him? Is there any way to see Him?

It's true that we can't see Jesus as we see each other, but the Bible lets us know how we can see Him. Have you ever seen anyone who needs help? *(Give examples: parents, friends.)* Do you know anyone who is sick and needs someone to take care of him? Do you know someone who needs clothes or food? Jesus tells us that when we help others, we are helping Him.

We see Jesus—and show Him to others—by the way we treat people. It can be hard to treat some people nicely. Some of us may have short tempers. You may be embarrassed by someone who is missing the right kind of clothes, and not want to share yours. You may be tired of having a brother or sister around all the time. No one feels like being helpful all the time.

Remember, others are looking at us and need to see Jesus in us. How should we act so they will see Jesus? *(Discuss.)*

Binoculars won't help people see Jesus. You will.

PRAYER: Help us to act in a way so that others will see Jesus when they see our actions. Amen.

BOUNCED

THEME: Give, and you will receive.

OBJECT: A basketball

TEXT: "Give, and you will receive. You will be given much. It will be poured into your hands—more than you can hold. You will be given so much that it will spill into your lap. The way you give to others is the way God will give to you." *Luke 6:38*

APPLICATION:

(Begin by bouncing a ball.) One of my favorite games is basketball. I like to watch others play, but I also like to play with the ball by myself. What makes a ball fun is that when you throw it against a wall, or on the floor, it bounces right back. *(Demonstrate.)* When we throw the ball against something, it comes right back.

The Bible speaks about getting back what we give away. When we do nice things for others, we will get good things back. The things that we get in return are not always things we can hold in our hands. Sometimes giving to others helps us to become less selfish—we receive the gift of generosity. Giving to others can make us feel good—we receive the gift of knowing we have made someone happy. Often we feel so good about giving that the good feeling is better than any other gift we could get in return. And sometimes, people respond to our gifts of kindness by being kind to us.

Don't go out and give just so you can get something. That's not what the Bible tells us to do. But know that giving can bring special joy. Like the ball returning to us, God promises to bless us as we have given.

PRAYER: Lord, may we know the joy of giving. Amen.

KEYED IN

THEME: Jesus—the only way

OBJECTS: Keys

TEXT: Jesus answered, "I am the way. And I am the truth and the life. The only way to the Father is through me."

John 14:6

APPLICATION:

Wait until you see all the keys I brought along today! I have car keys, a house key, and some other keys. A lot of things need to be opened with keys. If I come home without a key, I am locked out. If I don't have the right key to start my car, I'm going nowhere—especially if my key is inside my locked car.

Can I start my car with my house key? Can I get in my house with the car key? Of course not.

We can't get into Heaven without the right key either. No house key, or car key will help. Some think they can get into Heaven by being nice, especially to people they don't like. There are also people who believe that if they don't use bad words, they will have no problem getting in. Others think the way to go to Heaven is by going to church every week, and putting lots of money in the offering. But there is only one "key" to get into Heaven—Jesus. If we believe that Jesus Christ saved us when He died on the cross and we accept His gift of salvation, He is our key to eternal life— our only key.

PRAYER: Father, we thank You for making us part of Your family, and giving us Jesus—the key to get into our home in Heaven someday. Amen.

BE ATTACHED

THEME: We need God in our lives.

OBJECT: A recently cut branch, complete with leaves

TEXT: "I am the vine, and you are the branches. If a person remains in me and I remain in him, then he produces much fruit. But without me he can do nothing."

John 15:5

APPLICATION:

I brought a branch along today. You can see it's pretty big, but it may get even larger. I thought we'd just sit around here and watch it grow. Won't it be fun to see more branches grow out and many leaves sprout? Let's sit very quietly, and watch. *(Long pause.)*

Did anyone see it grow? Let's see: one, two, three—does it seem to have more leaves? Do you see any fruit? Why isn't it growing? I guess maybe if we just waited longer it would do something. No? Why not? *(Discuss.)*

You're right. The branch isn't growing because it is cut off from the tree. If you look closely you will see that some leaves have withered already. A longer wait wouldn't help. The leaves will just die and fall off.

A branch can't be healthy or bear fruit if it's cut off from the tree. The Bible tells us that we can't be fruitful if we're cut off from Jesus. What does that mean? Do you know what kinds of fruit trees have? *(Discuss—apples, pears, etc.)* What kind of fruit do people have? When we are called fruitful, it doesn't mean that we will have crisp apples, or juicy oranges grow out of our ears. We will have fruits like love, joy, peace, patience, and kindness. I want to have those fruits in my life. How about you?

We need to stay very close to Jesus, talking and learning. Then we'll be fruitful.

PRAYER: Father, help us to stay attached to Jesus, growing and being fruitful. Amen.

TEAMWORK

THEME: Working together

OBJECTS:
  A very large potato — Dictator
  A very small potato — Commentator
  Two matching potatoes — Imitators
  A potato with large specks on it — Spectator
  A sweet potato

TEXT: "This is my command: Love each other as I have
  loved you." *John 15:12*

APPLICATION:
  It is not easy for people, even Christians, to work
together as a team. I brought along some potatoes to show
how we are different. Some of us want to tell others what to
do. This bossy person is a *(pause before each word, with
emphasis on the first syllable)* dic-tator. *(Show large
potato.)* Older brothers and sisters can be dictators.
  Another person may not act like a show-off, but this
person has lots of little comments to say about everything.
This person is a comment-tator *(show small potato)*. Kids
can be commentators, even in the middle of a Sunday-
school class.
  Then there are those who only want to do what everyone
else is doing. *(Show identical potatoes.)* These potatoes
look alike. They're imi-tators. They say and do the same
things. Often they must wear the same kind of clothes as
everyone else too. Just as much a problem are those who
wish to be only spec-tators. *(Show potato with specks.)*
Spectators just watch everyone else do what needs to be
done. Sometimes they sit next to the commentator to make
sure he doesn't miss anything. *(Put the commentator next
to the spectator.)*
  Jesus gave us an example of how He wants us to act. We
are to love others just as He loves us. Love should be

shown through our actions.

The sweet potato looks much like other potatoes. *(Show.)* But inside it is a different color and has a sweeter taste. You have eyes, and hair, and look similar to other people around, but inside you are different. Christians must be filled with a sweet, kind, loving spirit.

(Hold the potatoes up as you speak of them.) Don't be bossy like a dictator. Make only good comments about others. God made you a special person. Instead of being an imitator, be as special as God made you to be. And then there's that hard one. The spectator just watches work being done. If we love others, we'll want to help clean up around the house and join in with doing the dishes. We will be first to help at church.

You are different. *(Hold up the sweet potato.)* Love others just as Jesus loves you. Teamwork is the result of that love.

PRAYER: Lord, help us to work together, because Jesus has shown us how to love. Amen.

THE BRIGHT SIDE

THEME: God makes good out of bad.

OBJECTS: A lemon, a knife

TEXT: We know that in everything God works for the good of those who love him. *Romans 8:28*

APPLICATION:
"Oh, go suck a lemon." Have you ever said that to anyone? I hope not. Usually you would say that to someone you were unhappy with, because what does a lemon taste like? *(Cut lemon and let someone try.)* It is very sour, isn't it? Not a wonderful snack. In fact, being "stuck with a lemon" means you have something worthless, or at least

with a lot of problems. At the same time, my very favorite drink is made with lemons—lemonade. With sweetening added, what was at first very sour becomes a most refreshing drink.

Sometimes in life bad things happen. Maybe a friend is nasty to you. Maybe you're sick just when you wanted to go somewhere special. Kids at school can be very mean.

The good news is that if we belong to Jesus, He is with us during difficult times. He promises that blessings come from what seem like impossible situations.

Just as lemons need something added to make them good, so our lives need Jesus. We can't always sit around waiting for Him to make things better. Like adding sugar to lemons, sometimes God uses us to make things happen. That may mean being the first to say you're sorry after you've had a fight, or spending extra hours working on a problem.

If we love God, He will bless what we do for Him.

PRAYER: Thank You for always being with us and making good come from times that are hard. Amen.

TRANSFORMED

THEME: The change Jesus Christ brings

OBJECTS: Two bags of microwave popcorn, one popped, one not. In some situations you can use just one bag and pop it during the demonstration in a microwave oven.

TEXT: Do not change yourselves to be like the people of this world. But be changed within by a new way of thinking. *Romans 12:2*

APPLICATION:
(Pick up unpopped bag.) I'm anxious to open this bag of

microwave popcorn so that I can share it with you. *(Begin to open.)* Nothing is better than beautiful, white, fluffy popcorn. That's strange. I wonder why it doesn't smell like popcorn. Wait a minute. Something is wrong. Look at this. *(Show inside of bag.)* It's a lumpy, gooey mess. Would you like to eat this? Yuck! No way. It's useless!

How come? I was all ready to eat popcorn. *(Let the group explain that something has to happen to it.)* For it to be used, it needs to go through a change. It's the heat that turns this mess into something good. *(Open and sniff the finished product.)* Just the smell makes others want to eat some.

Just as all popcorn needs to be changed before we can eat it, so all of us need to be changed before God can use us. On our own we are selfish and unkind. I have seen faces so sad that a bird could land on the bottom lip. *(Frown with bottom lip out.)* Is it fun to be around people like that? *(No.)* Until we are changed, we are as useless as this mess. *(Show unpopped corn.)*

Jesus can change us from useless, to useful. When He lives in our hearts, we become very different. *(Show popped corn.)* Jesus helps us be kind. We become happy when we can help others. The smiles on our faces make others want to know more about Jesus, just like the smell of fresh popcorn makes others want to have some.

(Show before and after popcorn.) What a difference! Only heat can change popcorn, and only Jesus can change us.

PRAYER: Lord, change our lives and make us happy, useful Christians. Amen.

WHAT YOU DO, DO WELL

THEME: We are each unique in God's kingdom.

OBJECTS: Ingredients of a sandwich, or shapes cut out of pieces of colored paper to resemble bread, lettuce, a slice of cheese, onion, tomato, ham, and mayonnaise.

TEXT: We all have different gifts. Each gift came because of the grace that God gave us.   *Romans 12:6*

APPLICATION:

I have a favorite sandwich. Each part of the sandwich is needed for it to be the best. *(Demonstrate.)* Between two slices of bread I add lettuce, cheese, onion, tomato, ham and mayonnaise—especially the mayonnaise. Without it, I might as well put all the other things back.

Just as my sandwich needs each part to make it good, our church needs people who are good at doing different things to make our church family the very best it can be.

We need people who are always helpful. Those who constantly say "let us (lettuce) help." *(Identify each ingredient as added.)* Then, of course, there are teachers who everyone is drawn to (cheese). You may still be stuck on some teacher you've had in the past. There are those who stand out as strong leaders (onion). They stick out in any crowd, and may not be easy to get close to. That's why we have loving people who share everything, and make everyone feel at home (tomato). To help us work, we have friends who are fun to be around (ham). They keep everyone happy and laughing. But without God's love (mayonnaise), we might as well forget it. His love is what makes everything else work together.

God makes each of us special, and when we all do our part, our church family is at its best.

PRAYER: Lord, we are all different, but help us to remember that each of us is good at something needed in Your church. Amen.

HARMONIZE

THEME: Unity

OBJECTS: A saw and a potted plant with thick branches

TEXT: Live together in peace with each other . . . . Do your best to live in peace with everyone.   *Romans 12:16, 18*

APPLICATION:

I brought along my saw and a plant. Let's begin cutting this beautiful branch. Notice what happens as I cut. I'm making a mark on the wood. It's not a very pretty mark. In fact, the branch is badly damaged just by cutting through the bark. If I keep sawing, this branch will break off.

Something else happens after I do lots of sawing—the saw gets dull. If I'm not careful, it can get so dull and rusty that it is no longer useful.

Just as I can hurt a branch, it is possible to hurt other people. Have you ever hurt someone? How? *(Discuss hurts, leading to inside hurts.)* Sometimes we say nasty things that make others feel bad. Those nasty words can cut people and make them hurt. If we are mean enough, we can make someone look and feel very sad.

What happens to us when we are mean to others? When we hurt others, we also hurt ourselves. An unkind persons does not keep many friends. Instead of cutting words, use words that make others feel good about themselves. Try to get along well with others. Be kind. The Bible calls that living "in harmony."

A branch looks better without ugly marks. You will feel better when you get along with others.

PRAYER: May we be careful not to hurt others and ourselves, by the things we say and do. Amen.

REFLECTING JESUS

THEME: Become like Jesus.

OBJECT: Mirror

TEXT: We can be mirrors that brightly reflect the glory of the Lord. And as the Spirit of the Lord works within us, we become more and more like him.

2 Corinthians 3:18, TLB

APPLICATION:

Look at this mirror. Don't you just love it? Sometimes a mirror gets very bright, and makes light shine in other places in the room. What can I do to make this mirror shine? Just a minute. Let me see if I can plug it in to make it work. *(Look around for an electrical outlet.)* Do I need electricity to make this mirror shine? What is needed? A mirror reflects any light that shines on it. Look how when the ceiling light shines on it, I can make it reflect light around the room, even though the mirror has no power of its own.

The Bible tells us we can be mirrors that reflect God's glory. By ourselves we don't shine, any more than the mirror can be bright without light to reflect. The only way we can shine is when we are close to Jesus. When we let ourselves reflect Him, we become more like Him.

If we are mirrors of Jesus, how will we act? *(Discuss the things we will do if we are mirroring Jesus: helping others, building others up, obeying, being thankful and loving.)*

Let's pray that we can be mirrors reflecting Jesus.

PRAYER: Lord, may our lives reflect You more each day. Amen.

IN THE BAG

THEME: Troubles make us strong.

OBJECTS: Tea bag, cup, cold water

TEXT: I am very happy to brag about my weaknesses. Then Christ's power can live in me. So I am happy when I have weaknesses, insults, hard times, sufferings, and all kinds of troubles. All these things are for Christ. And I am happy, because when I am weak, then I am truly strong.
2 Corinthians 12:9, 10

APPLICATION:
Sometimes I get thirsty at the strangest times—like right now. Good thing I have a tea bag along with me. I'll add some water, and I can enjoy a thirst-quenching drink. *(Fill cup with water.)* Hmm. It's a little slow to turn the right color. Maybe I can squeeze it against the side of the cup with the spoon. *(Look inside.)* That didn't seem to do it.

Help me. How can I make some tea? *(Need hot water.)* It's true that if you just float the bag around in cool water, it doesn't make a good drink. How hot does the water have to be? To make good tea, the water has to be boiling—so hot that it would hurt your finger if you dunked it in. Even to make iced tea, you need hot water first, and then cool it. The very thing that hurts so much is the only thing that makes the tea useful.

Life is like that. Sometimes bad things happen to us. Just as the tea bag is dipped in boiling water, we may have things happen to us that hurt. We may lose a good friend, or be injured somehow—maybe even by someone. Perhaps we are hurt when a favorite toy is broken. We hurt for a long time.

Just as a tea bag becomes useful when put in hot water, Jesus can use bad things in our lives to make us better boys and girls. When bad things happen, we often get to know Jesus better because we are reminded of how much we need Him. We can see that only His strength gets us through. Others can see God's power in our lives. Sometimes only those who have had bad things happen to them can help others who get hurt in the same way.

We may not know why certain things happen to us, but we can know that God can take bad experiences and turn them into good.

Hot water makes strong tea. Hard times show us God's strength.

PRAYER: We praise You, Lord. The hard things that happen to us help us know You better. Amen.

BLACK OR WHITE

THEME: Results of bad language

OBJECT: Black licorice

TEXT: When you talk, do not say harmful things. But say what people need—words that will help others become stronger. Then what you say will help those who listen to you.   *Ephesians 4:29*

APPLICATION:
Even those who love the taste of licorice may not like what happens when they eat it. *(Put a piece in your mouth.)* What happens when you have black licorice in your mouth? *(Chew and open your mouth.)* A mouth that has eaten licorice is a black mouth. Not only does your tongue look horrible, soon your teeth, and even your lips get black. Yuck! If you drool a little and it falls on your shirt, it's hard to remove the stain. It takes a while before your mouth is a normal color, and until then, you better keep it shut.

Did you know that the Bible talks about our mouths, and the words we speak? We're not to use bad language.

Remember that such talk has a lasting effect. Like licorice leaves our mouths black for a long time, we can see the results of bad words long after they are spoken. Not only do they make us look bad, but they can hurt others too. Once a bad or unkind word comes out, it usually leaves an ugly mark, much like a bad spot on my shirt.

Use words that build each other up. What words make people feel good? *(Good job, I love you, compliments.)* Licorice leaves an ugly mess in our mouths. Using bad language can leave a mess in our lives that is just as ugly. If we can't say anything good, it's better to keep our mouths closed.

PRAYER: Lord, may our words always be kind and helpful. Amen.

FEET FOR LIFE

THEME: Be quick to share Christ.

OBJECTS: Heavy boots or hip boots, running shoes, Bible

TEXT: Wear shoes that are able to speed you on as you preach the Good News of peace with God.

Ephesians 6:15, TLB

APPLICATION:
I thought I'd come ready to go for a run, but I had trouble picking out what to wear on my feet. I wore these boots, so I'd be ready for anything. I can go through rain, snow and sleet. My feet will stay dry. What do you think? Are these perfect for a run down the road? *(Pause.)* No? Why not? *(Slow, clumsy, etc.)* I guess you're right. *(Take off the boots.)* Wearing these boots would not be a good idea. I might fall, or worse yet, be embarrassed.

Good thing for me, I brought my trusty running shoes.

Do these look like a better choice? Check out the tread—perfect to get a good grip on the road. In fact, some of the road is still stuck in the tread. They're much lighter than the boots. *(Compare weight, one in each hand.)* You can't see it, but inside the soles are pads of gel (or soft pads), so each step is cushioned. Even the color is better than the boots, and they have some reflectors on them so that I won't get run over by a car at night. Anyone would want to have shoes like these!

To be ready to run, we slip into running shoes. To be ready to tell about Jesus, we need to study the Bible. *(Hold up.)* Nothing else can prepare us as well to tell our friends about Jesus. It's hard to tell others about Jesus if we don't know Him well. The Bible helps us know Him well. We won't be clumsy like walking in heavy boots, or embarrassed by not being prepared.

We can be quick and ready. Even young boys and girls can tell people about God if they know what the Bible says. They won't have to take the time to ask a parent or teacher.

Be quick to share the good news that Jesus can help us. Get ready. Learn what the Bible teaches.

PRAYER: Help us to listen in church and Sunday school, and to study the Bible, so we will be ready to tell our friends about Jesus. Amen.

KEEPING ON

THEME: God is steadfast.

OBJECTS: Dandelions

TEXT: And I am sure that God who began the good work within you will keep right on helping you grow in his grace until his task within you is finally finished on that day when Jesus Christ returns.   *Philippians 1:6, TLB*

APPLICATION:
It always has been hard for me to get pretty green grass to grow in my yard. Where people walk, the ground gets hard. If it doesn't rain often enough, the grass gets brown.

There is something that I can get to grow in my yard every year—dandelions. Hot or cold, rain or shine, the yellow "flowers" cover my yard. Once they start to grow they multiply quickly with little gray seeds that blow in the wind. If I try to pull them out, the root may break off, and if I don't get the root out, the plant doesn't die.

Dandelions are weeds, but we can learn a lot from them. As Christians we should stand our ground firmly and multiply quickly when we tell others about Jesus. God keeps on helping us make this happen.

Almost nothing can destroy dandelions, but if you pick one and it's no longer attached to its root, it wilts quickly, as you can see by my not-so-pretty bouquet. This is also a lesson for us. As long as we are "rooted" in God's Word and praying every day, we stay strong. When we stay close to God, we grow and are able to finish whatever work He has for us. That's a promise—God's promise.

PRAYER Thank You, God, that we can get strength from being close to You. Amen.

STAR BRIGHT

THEME: Complaining

OBJECT: A paper star

TEXT: Do everything without complaining or arguing. Then you will be innocent and without anything wrong in you. You will be God's children without fault. But you are living with crooked and mean people all around you. Among them you shine like stars in the dark world.

Philippians 2:14, 15

APPLICATION:

I've cut a star out of paper, but it doesn't look much like the real thing. Sit outside on a very clear night and watch all the beautiful stars. They all shine so brightly that you can see them clearly from very far away.

The Bible tells us that we can be like stars to those around us. How do you think we must act so we can shine like stars? *(Get suggestions.)* I guess I'd shine like a star if I kept my room clean, or helped clear the table after eating. The Bible tells us we'll shine like stars if we do everything without complaining or arguing. That's hard. On the other hand, it might be easier to clean my room than to keep complaining.

Do you ever complain or argue? You may fight with your brother or sister, or complain when you have to do chores around the house. Maybe you don't like to be reminded to do your homework. God's Word tells us not to complain or argue. If we don't, we'll shine as brightly as stars in a dark sky. That means when others complain, our happiness will make us stand out for all to know we belong to Jesus.

PRAYER: We want to shine for You by not complaining or arguing. May we be happy Christians. Amen.

DEALING WITH DOLLARS

THEME: What to do with money

OBJECT: A dollar bill

TEXT: Give this command to those who are rich with things of this world. Tell them not to be proud. Tell them to hope in God, not their money. Money cannot be trusted, but God takes care of us richly. He gives us everything to enjoy. Tell the rich people to do good and to be rich in doing good deeds. Tell them to be happy to give and ready to share. *1 Timothy 6:17, 18*

APPLICATION:

Look what I brought along to teach us about money. Can you all see what this is? *(Dollar.)* All of us know how to spend money. Do we all need money? What do we use our money for? *(Discuss needs and wants.)*

Some people may think the Bible teaches that money is bad. That's not true. You see, I can have this dollar bill in my hand *(hold money away from you)*, but it doesn't block my vision of the world around. I can still see friends, see people who may need my help, see work to be done, see God's Word, and see the cross in front of our church.

The problem comes only if I hold the money too close to me. *(Hold the dollar tightly in front of your eyes.)* This happens if I love money too much. That love leads to all kinds of trouble. I can no longer see my friends, or those who need hugs. I can't see the Bible, or any reminders of Jesus Christ who died for me.

Having money is not the problem. But if I love money too much—and hold it too close—it can become a problem. Remember, it is God who gives us everything, and we should use everything, including our money, to do good. What are some good things to do with money?

PRAYER: Thank You for money. Help us to remember to do good things with it. Amen.

PERFECT VISION

THEME: Infallible Scriptures

OBJECT: A pair of glasses without lenses

TEXT: All Scripture is given by God and is useful for teaching and for showing people what is wrong in their lives. It is useful for correcting faults and teaching how to live right. *2 Timothy 3:16*

APPLICATION:

How do you like my new glasses? *(Put on.)* They look pretty good on me now, but I didn't like them at all when I first got them. For one thing, I got tired of cleaning all the dirty spots off the glass. They were also heavy, and they left horrible marks on my nose. The biggest problem was that when my friends took pictures of me, the pictures showed a big white reflection of the camera's flashbulb right where my beautiful eyes should be!

So I changed them. *(Make it obvious that there are no lenses.)* This way they are easier to clean *(demonstrate cleaning the frames),* lightweight *(toss around a bit),* and my eyes show up in pictures *(put on and show a big smile).*

(With continued smile.) There is one very small problem. *(Smile disappears.)* Actually, kind of a very BIG problem. *(Pause.)* You guessed it. I can't see. I still wear the glasses all the time. The only thing I did was take the glass out—a teeny, tiny change, but now I can't see.

I took the lens out of my glasses. Some people take things out of God's Word. This is especially true when it comes to the commandments God gives in His Word. We usually leave in the commandment not to steal, and certainly the one about not killing anyone. Still, I know kids who are totally bummed because their parents will not buy a certain pair of basketball shoes that someone else has. God tells us not to want what other have, or be jealous. He also tells us to obey and honor our parents. Are we honoring our mothers if they have to tell us ten times to clean our room? When we disobey just one of the rules of God, He tells us we have broken them all (James 2:10). We can't pick and choose, because every part of the Bible is important.

You can't change the Bible to make it easy on yourself, to lighten up the message, or to make yourself look better. God's whole Word teaches us what we need to know to live for Him.

PRAYER: Lord, thank You for the Bible, Your guide for our lives. Amen.

GROW UP

THEME: Nonconformity

OBJECT: A chameleon (can be a picture)

TEXT: That is the way we should live, because God's grace has come. That grace can save every person. It teaches us not to live against God and not to do the evil things the world wants to do. That grace teaches us to live on earth now in a wise and right way—a way that shows that we serve God. *Titus 2:11, 12*

APPLICATION:
The chameleon is an interesting little lizard. If you watch him carefully, you will see that he changes color to blend in with the colors around him. Most people believe that he does this for protection. Enemies can't pester him if they can't see him.

I can't help but think how much we are like that little lizard. We want to blend in with everything and everyone around. So often it is very important to wear clothes similar to others, and act like those we are with. Like the chameleon, we often change to match those we are with. We talk one way when we are at church, and another when we are with friends who don't go to church.

One way to show we are growing up is to choose to do right. Some things are wrong. We have a choice. We can say no when asked to do wrong things. We can choose to believe what the Bible tells us rather than believe those who lie to us. It's easier to be one of the crowd, and go along with what others do. Standing alone doesn't feel as safe, so we may be tempted, like the chameleon, to try and match who we are with. But Christian children and adults must learn to stand alone. The chameleon changes color to blend in. We are called by God to be different.

PRAYER: Lord, give us Your protection as we take a stand for You. Amen.

LIFE SAVERS

THEME: Christ, our lifesaver

OBJECT: Life Savers candy

TEXT: Jesus lives forever. He will never stop serving as priest. So he is always able to save those who come to God through him. He can do this, because he always lives, ready to help those who come before God.

Hebrews 7:24, 25

APPLICATION:

The other day, as I was sucking on one of these little candies, I was thinking about what a great help they are to me. After eating a pepperoni pizza these are very helpful to sweeten my breath. They also help if I get a coughing spell right in the middle of a Sunday worship service. Few things work as well as these. In fact, they are so helpful, what do we call them? *(Life Savers.)* They do seem to save our lives. If you have a smelly mouth, or if you can't stop coughing, they are the answer.

There are problems with these Life Savers. They are pretty small in the first place, and then they have holes in them. They don't last long. Soon after they've melted down to that thin ring, they disappear. Then your sweet breath may disappear and your cough may come back.

The Bible tells about a permanent lifesaver. That lifesaver is Jesus Christ, and because He lives forever, He is a permanent help. The Life Savers candy helps me get closer to those I'm talking to. Jesus is there to make it possible for me to get close to God.

We don't always do things right and God is a perfect Lord. I'm glad we have Jesus as our lifesaver. He connects us to God. He is perfect. Through Him, our sins are forgiven, and we have eternal life.

PRAYER: Candy Life Savers don't last. Thank You for giving us a permanent lifesaver in Jesus Christ. Amen.

LIGHTEN UP

THEME: Positive thinking

OBJECT: Dark sunglasses

TEXT: Let us look only to Jesus. He is the one who began our faith, and he makes our faith perfect. Jesus suffered death on the cross. But he accepted the shame of the cross as if it were nothing. He did this because of the joy that God put before him. And now he is sitting at the right side of God's throne.   *Hebrews 12:2*

APPLICATION:
(Enter wearing dark glasses.) It is really dark in here. Really dark. The ceiling is dark, the windows are kind of dark, and all of you look kind of dark. I wonder why that is. *(Someone will respond that you have on dark glasses.)* Oh, I guess that's true. I don't really need these glasses. I just left them on because it was easier than taking them off.

That may seem kind of silly to you, but did you ever know someone who talked as if they *always* had on dark glasses? They are not fun to be around. They look on the dark side of everything. He or she is sad because it might rain tomorrow. Even at church they feel bad they aren't dressed just right. For some people, it's easier to stay unhappy than to work to make things better.

If you're like that, it's time to look at Jesus. He allowed many bad things to happen to Him so that we could learn to keep trying when bad things happen to us. He was even willing to die on the cross because He knew the joy that was waiting for Him in Heaven. What an example for us! Don't let small things keep you from remembering the joy we have because we belong to a wonderful God. Don't look on the dark side. Look up to the light.

PRAYER: Thank You for the joy we have when we fix our eyes on You. Amen.

BE SPOTLESS

THEME: Purity

OBJECTS: A clear, clean drinking glass and a dirty glass with spots

TEXT: But God made a promise to us. And we are waiting for what he promised—a new heaven and a new earth where goodness lives. Dear friends, we are waiting for this to happen. So try as hard as you can to be without sin and without fault.   *2 Peter 3:13, 14*

APPLICATION:
Do you know how to wash dishes? Oh, don't get upset. I didn't ask if you wanted to do dishes, only if you knew how to do dishes. It's important to wash with hot, soapy water, and then rinse everything well—especially the glasses. If I don't do it right, they can still look dirty and full of spots *(show dirty glass).* You can see how this glass still looks grubby, has spots and lipstick stuck to the rim. Does it look like a glass you would want to use? *(No.)* If my washed glass looks like this, I've got to start over.

The only thing worse than doing dishes, is doing dishes a second time. That takes time, but the dishes all look much better when I'm finished and we can use them.

The Bible doesn't talk about spotty glasses, but did you know that it tells us that we can be spotty? When we think or say things that are wrong, we are no longer bright, spotless Christians. Asking God to forgive us is like being washed. God cleans us and lets us start over.

We must try with God's help to live without sinning. When we do sin, we need to tell God we are sorry. He forgives, and helps us clean up our lives. Pray for God's help in being a sparkling-clean Christian.

PRAYER: God, thank You for forgiving us and helping us to live clean lives that please You. Amen.

KNOW IT—SHOW IT

THEME: Our actions show that we belong to Jesus.

OBJECT: A hospital ID bracelet

TEXT: Little children, let us stop just saying we love people; let us really love them, and show it by our actions. Then we will know for sure, by our actions, that we are on God's side. *1 John 3:18, 19, TLB*

APPLICATION:
Today I'm wearing a bracelet. It is not a pretty bracelet, but it has a purpose. This one was given to me by a hospital. You get one if you are a patient. If you wear it, the doctors and nurses know which medicines and operations to give you to help you get well. The bracelet also shows everyone that you belong in the hospital, and who your doctor is.

When we give our lives to Jesus, He doesn't give us a wristband to wear. He knows each of us by name, and knows exactly what we need to make us better. How do other people know that we belong to Jesus? *(Discuss actions.)*

The Bible tells us that it should be very easy to tell who belongs to Jesus, because Christians love others. This is a scary thought. Does this mean we have to love even brothers who smell bad, or sisters who scream at us? Yup. Can you think of any other ways we could act, or things we could do to show love? *(Get suggestions.)*

We need to love others so much that they will know right away that we are Christians, and that it is Jesus who takes care of us.

PRAYER: May others know we are Christians, and belong to Jesus by the way we love others. Amen.

IN BETWEEN

THEME: Jesus, the mediator

OBJECT: An appliance with a three-prong electrical cord, an electrical adapter changing three prongs to two, an outlet for two prongs

TEXT: God has given us eternal life, and this life is in his Son. Whoever has the Son has life. But the person who does not have the Son of God does not have life.

1 John 5:11, 12

APPLICATION:

What would we do without electricity? Our families use it every day for many appliances. Sometimes it is not possible to plug into the power. Not long ago I wanted to clean the floor with a vacuum cleaner, and found out that the three-prong plug wouldn't fit into my wall socket, because the wall socket had only two holes.

I needed what is called an adapter. See how this little gadget goes between my cord and the plug and lets the cord get the power? Without the adapter, I couldn't clean with my vacuum cleaner.

Just as my vacuum couldn't plug into the power source without the adapter, my only way to get power from God is through Jesus Christ. Jesus died so sins could be cleaned away and we could be close to God. He stands between me and God the Father, making eternal life possible. That means He is our mediator.

He is the way, the truth and the life.

PRAYER: Dear God, thank You for giving me Jesus to be my way to get power and eternal life. Amen.